Ji-Nongo-Nongo
MEANS RIDDLES

JI-NONGO-NONGO MEANS RIDDLES

by VERNA AARDEMA   illustrated by JERRY PINKNEY

FOUR WINDS PRESS

NEW YORK

MEDIA CENTER
White Brook Middle School
200 Park Street
Easthampton, MA 01027

ESEA Title IV

For reprint permission, grateful acknowledgment is made to:

Adam and Charles Black for three riddles from *The Essential Kafir,* by Dudley Kidd.

Funk and Wagnalls Publishing Company, Inc., for two riddles from *Funk & Wagnalls Standard Dictionary of Folklore, Mythology, and Legend,* edited by Maria Leach, copyright, © 1949 by Funk & Wagnalls Publishing Company, Inc.

Horizon Press for a riddle from *Yes and No, The Intimate Folklore of Africa* by Alta Jablow, © 1961 by Alta Jablow.

Macmillan & Company for a riddle from *Liberian Folklore* by Doris Banks Henries.

Oxford University Press for four riddles from *The Masai, Their Language and Folklore,* by Claud Hollis, and for eleven riddles from *Hausa Folk-lore, Customs, Proverbs, Etc.,* by Robert Sutherland Rattray.

Seeley, Service & Cooper, Ltd., for four riddles from *Wild Bush Tribes of Tropical Africa,* by G. Cyril Claridge.

Library of Congress Cataloging in Publication Data

Aardema, Verna.
  Ji-nongo-nongo means riddles.

  Bibliography: p.
  Summary: Presents a collection of riddles from Africa.
  1. Riddles, African—Juvenile literature.
  [1. Riddles] I. Pinkney, Jerry. II. Title.
  PN6371.5.A25   398.6'096   78–4038
            ISBN 0–590–07474–1

Published by Four Winds Press
A division of Scholastic Magazines, Inc., New York, N.Y.
Library of Congress Catalog Card Number: 78–4038
1 2 3 4 5   82 81 80 79 78

This is my answer to Boys and Girls

—they asked *me* riddles when I was a teacher.

By the same author

Tales from the Story Hat
Tales for the Third Ear
Behind the Back of the Mountain
Why Mosquitoes Buzz in People's Ears
Who's in Rabbit's House?

JI-NONGO-NONGO
✦ MEANS RIDDLES ✦

Congo

Who can trust his money to a monkey?
Answer: The man who can climb trees.

Congo

Who can whistle with another man's mouth?
Answer: The other man.

Yoruba

When will a man not go to bed, even though it is night?
Answer: When his house is on fire.

Yoruba

When does a man run through thorn bushes?
Answer: When something is chasing him.

Congo

What can a dog do that a man can not?
Answer: Lick his own back.

Congo

Why shouldn't you grow pumpkins on the side of a hill?
Answer: Because when they are ripe, they would roll down.

Yoruba

What does the pig do after wallowing in the mud?
Answer: He looks for a clean person to rub against.

Yoruba

What does the pin say to the kente cloth?
Answer: Don't hang your troubles on my neck!

Yoruba

What thing in the forest frightens even the lion?
Answer: The forest fire.

Yoruba

Who is the long thin trading woman who never reaches the market?

Answer: The canoe left at the landing, while its owner goes on to the market.

Accra

When is it safe to play with the leopard cubs?
Answer: When their mother is far away.

Krahn

How does one cure a bad sore?
Answer: With a bad medicine.

Yoruba

Who has a house too small for guests?
Answer: The tortoise.

Ga

What is soft and flat, but cannot be slept upon?
Answer: The surface of the lake.

Ga

What leaps down the mountain, but cannot climb back
up?
Answer: The mountain stream.

Yoruba

What can the buffalo do that two strong men can not?
Answer: Grow horns.

Yoruba

What is ugly when young and beautiful when full-grown?
Answer: The grub that becomes a butterfly.

Yoruba

What is long and can be shortened by the feet, but not
    with a hatchet?
Answer: The path.

Ga

What is it that you look at with one eye, but never with two?

Answer: The inside of a bottle.

Yoruba

They cut off its head. They cut off its feet. And its middle calls the town together. What is it?

Answer: A drum.

Oji

Bush-pig dies, Mangudu eats him. Kudu dies, Mangudu eats him. Mangudu dies, nobody eats him! Who is Mangudu?

Answer: The cooking pot.

Accra

Why does a boy poke a stick into a snake hole?
Answer: Because he wouldn't dare to put his hand into it.

Hausa

What looks at the valley, but never goes into it?
Answer: The hill.

Wolof

What is long but has no shadow?
Answer: The road.

Kanuri

What is it that even the ostrich with its long neck and
  sharp eyes cannot see?
Answer: What will happen tomorrow.

Masai

What doesn't run from the prairie fire?
Answer: The bare spot.

Masai

I have two skins—one to lie upon and the other to cover
  me. What are they?
Answer: The ground and the sky.

Wolof

When does the mouse say, "Nye, nye, nye!" to the cat?
Answer: When her hole is near.

Kafir

Who is the quiet little boy who is dressed at night and left
bare in the daytime?
Answer: The clothes peg.

Kafir

What is the longest snake in the world?
Answer: The road.

Wolof

What kind of tree cannot shade you?
Answer: One that is smaller than you are.

Hausa

What can make the woodcutter throw down his ax?
Answer: The little biting ants that fall from the tree.

Hausa

What lies down when it's hungry and stands up when
  it's full?
Answer: A rice sack.

Masai

What does a cow say when it is about to be sold?
Answer: "Strike a hard bargain! For the man who pays a
long price will treat me well."

Hausa

When do you pat the cow?
Answer: Before you milk her.

Hausa

Who doesn't get lost in the forest in the daytime?
Answer: The person who doesn't get lost there at night.

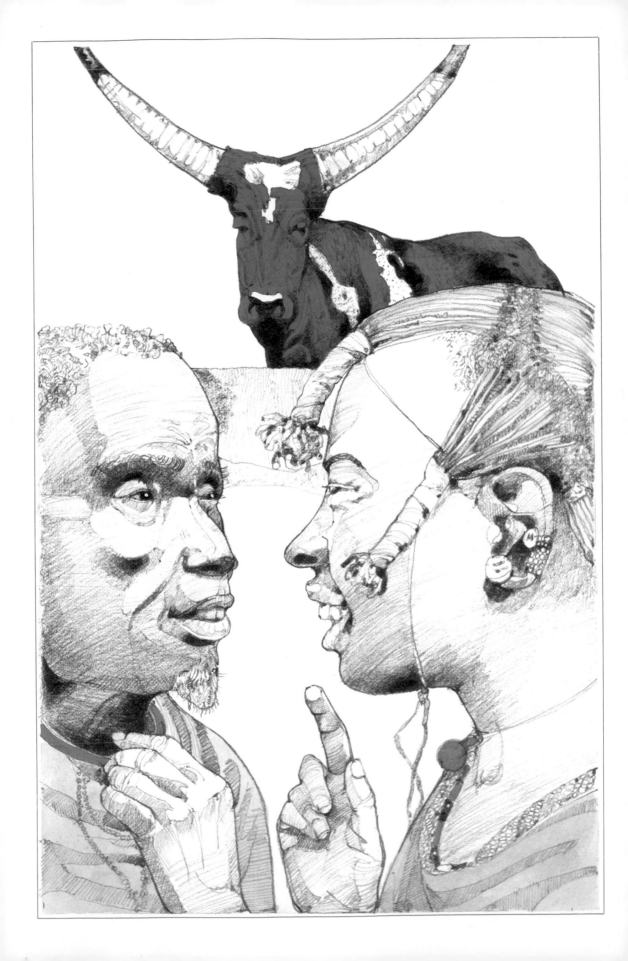

Masai

Who has more courage than a Masai warrior?
Answer: Two Masai warriors.

Hausa

Who won't listen when you tell him to stop?
Answer: The child who has never had a spanking.

Hausa

When do the mice play in the corn bin?
Answer: When the cat is not around.

Hausa

Why is a man like a pepper?
Answer: Until you have tested him, you can't tell how
    strong he is.

Kafir

Who is it that always stands, and never sits down?
Answer: A tree.

Hausa

What sleeping creature should never be touched?
Answer: The scorpion, because its stinging tail never
    sleeps.

Hausa

If the chief commands everyone to weep and fill a
      calabash with tears, what does the person with one
      eye do?

Answer: He weeps twice as hard.

Hausa

When does the hen fear the hawk?

Answer: When she has baby chicks.

Bibliography

Burton, Richard R. *Wit and Wisdom of West Africa.* London: Tinsley Brothers, 1865.

Claridge, Cyril. *Wild Bush Tribes of Tropical Africa.* London: Seeley, Service and Company, 1922.

Henries, Doris Banks. *Liberian Folklore.* London: Macmillan & Co., Ltd., 1966

Hollis, Claud. *The Masai, Their Language and Folklore.* London: Oxford at the Clarendon Press, 1905.

Jablow, Alta. *Yes and No, The Intimate Folklore of Africa.* New York: Horizon Press, 1961.

Kidd, Dudley. *The Essential Kafir.* London: Adam and Charles Black, 1904.

Leach, Maria, ed. *Standard Dictionary of Folklore, Mythology, and Legend.* Vol. I. New York: Funk and Wagnalls, 1949.

Lobagola, Bata Kindai Amgoza Ibn. *Folktales of a Savage.* London: Alfred A. Knopf, 1930.

Rattray, Robert S. *Hausa Folk-Lore, Customs, Proverbs, Etc.* Vol. II. London: Oxford at the Clarendon Press, 1913.

Notes

The source for the riddles from the Accra is *Wit and Wisdom of West Africa.*

The source for the riddles from the Congo is *Wild Bush Tribes of Tropical Africa.*

The source for the riddles from the Ga is *Wit and Wisdom of West Africa.*

The source for the riddles from the Hausa is *Hausa Folk-Lore, Customs, Proverbs, Etc.*

The source for the riddles from the Kafir is *The Essential Kafir.*

The source for the riddles from the Kanuri is *Wit and Wisdom of West Africa.*

The source for the riddles from the Krahn is *Liberian Folklore.*

The source for the riddles from the Masai is *The Masai, Their Language and Folklore.*

The source for the riddles from the Oji is *Wit and Wisdom of West Africa.*

The source for the riddles from the Wolof is *Wit and Wisdom of West Africa.*

The source for the riddle from the Yoruba on p. 2 is *Yes and No, The Intimate Folklore of Africa.*

The source for the riddles from the Yoruba on p. 14 is *Standard Dictionary of Folklore, Mythology, and Legend.*

The source for the riddles from the Yoruba on pp. 4, 6, 8, 10, and 12 is *Wit and Wisdom of West Africa.*

398.6   Aardema, Verna.
AAR
           Ji-nongo-nongo means
           riddles.
                              6.25

398.6   Aardema, Verna.
AAR   Ji-nongo-nongo
         means riddles.

DATE DUE

JUN. 1 4 1993		
Lassiter		
APR. 1 5 1997		